CELEBRATE   REC

UNIFY   DEFEND

N   EDUCATE   POWE

CHOOSE

E   CHALLENGE   CH

GENERATE   ILLUSTRATE

IMPLEMENT

PROMOTE   IMPROVE

LEAD   CONN

CONSTRUCT   MOTIVAT

QUESTION   S

CHAMPION   RESOLVE

CONNECT   CREA

RESIST   SOLVE   SPE

HOOSE   EMPOWER

TRANSFORM   EN

DEFEND   SERVE

DUCATE   IMPROVE

SOLVE INSPIRE
INSPIRE BOLSTER
GENERATE QUEST
OSE HONOR
IMPROVE RESTO
LLENGE CREATE
CELEBRATE RECOGNIZE
UNIFY DEFEND
ELEVATE CARE
URAGE ESTABLISH
TRANSFORM STAND
ERATE ILLUSTRATE
IMPLEMENT LEAD
PROMOTE INSPIRE
SUADE QUESTION
INVENT DEFY
CONSTRUCT MOTIVATE
ION RESOLVE

Nasty Woman

A JOURNAL

Anna Katz

Bluestreak
BOOKS

≡Bluestreak

Weldon Owen is a division of Bonnier Publishing USA
1045 Sansome Street, San Francisco, CA 94111
www.weldonowen.com

Copyright 2017 Weldon Owen Inc.

Edited and designed by Girl Friday Productions
www.girlfridayproductions.com

Written by Anna Katz

Illustration on page 50 used by permission of the artist. © Joanna Price.

Library of Congress Cataloging in Publication data is available.

ISBN-13: 978-1-68188-285-7

First Printed in 2017
10 9 8 7 6 5 4 3 2 1
2017 2018 2019 2020

Printed in China

Introduction

Let's not mince words: we have entered a full-on nightmare. An alternative reality where up is down and facts are subjective. A terrifying regression to an open-door policy for bigotry, jingoism, and -you guessed it—pussy grabbing.

This is not normal. Intolerance is not normal. Bans on immigrants and refugees are not normal. Mass incarceration is not normal. Restrictions on health care access and education are not normal. Antichoice is not normal. No, you can't pray the gay away, and climate change *is* happening. Just ask a polar bear.

If you're reading this, it's likely that you object to fraud or fat shaming or tax evasion or Russian hacking. Perhaps for you, civil rights violations and sexual assault allegations (and boasts) are deal breakers. As the Women's March on Washington and sister marches clearly demonstrated on January 21, 2017, you are not alone. No matter how heart-wrenching, disappointing, confusing, and soul-crushing the 2016 election season and its outcomes were, we have shown unambiguously that we will not take steps backward, that we will not keep quiet or go without a fight, that we will not take this lying down. We are paying attention, and we are mad as hell.

We may not yet have a woman in the Oval Office, but more than ever, women are in positions of power. And yet we still have plenty of work to do. Fortunately, there are many excellent role models—Nasty Women and Bad Hombres who have put up the good fight before us and who have worn whatever version of pussy hat was called for. In this journal are their words to inspire you and fortify you when times get tough. There is space for you to write your observations, thoughts, and feelings, using the prompts provided or just going freestyle. You'll also find a place for you to write your plans, because now is the time to not just reflect but *act*. To help you get started, there are tips for activism throughout, as well as a list of organizations and resources you can immediately support.

Someday a Nasty Woman will lead this nation—will lead this world. Because FUCK. THE. PATRIARCHY. Because women's rights are human rights. Because, at the end of even the darkest day, love wins.

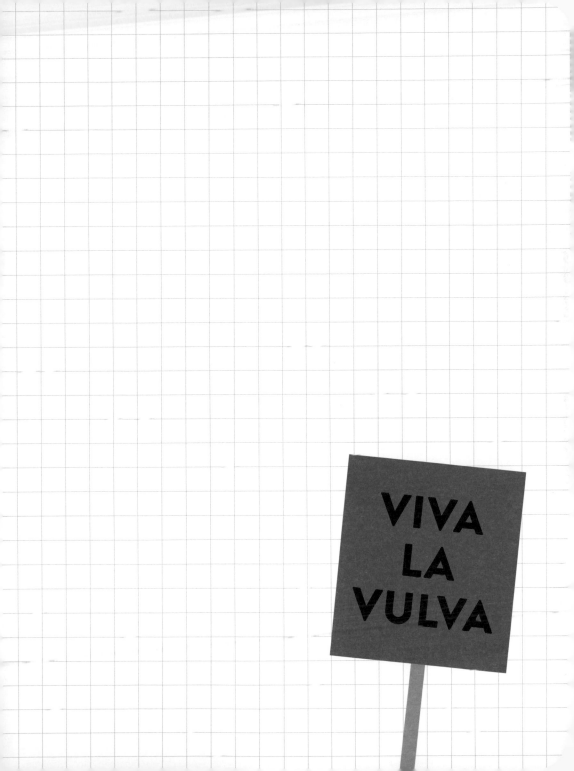

If there were one injustice you could solve with a snap of the fingers, what would it be? Why would you choose that one above all others?

CHANGE IS POSSIBLE—IF YOU FIGHT FOR IT.

Elizabeth Warren (b. 1949), US senator

I will not bow down to somebody else's whim or to someone else's ignorance.

bell hooks (b. 1952), author and social activist speaking
about playwright and African slave Publius Terentius Afer,
who lived and wrote in Rome, 1st century BCE

"Respect existence or expect resistance."

Sign at one of the women's marches, 1/21/2017

What is your greatest fear for yourself?

What is your greatest fear for your community?

66

I have been broken . . .
You have no idea what
I can take.

99

Roxane Gay (b. 1974),
writer, professor, and
commentator

> **"**
> *Power's not given to you.*
> *You have to take it.*
> **"**

Beyoncé Knowles-Carter
(b. 1981), singer and actor

How have you internalized societal messages about a group to which you belong? What messages about your race, religion, gender, class, etc., do you believe to be true? What messages do you believe to be false?

Black Lives
Matter.

> **"**
>
> (a) Do you have a vagina? and
> (b) Do you want to be in charge of it?
> If you said 'yes' to both, then
> congratulations! You're a feminist.
>
> **"**
>
> Caitlin Moran (b. 1975),
> author and journalist

Write about a time in your life when you may have behaved in a misogynistic way or experienced misogynistic behavior. Describe your thoughts, feelings, and actions in detail.

"

I will not be triumphed over.

"

Cleopatra (69–30 BCE),
pharaoh of Egypt

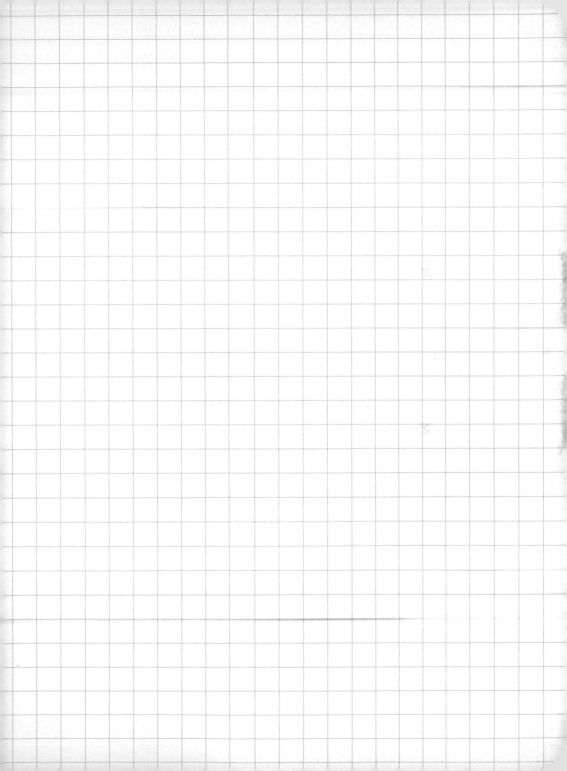

IMAGINE WAKING UP IN THE MORNING AS A DIFFERENT RACE OR SEX.

How would your life be different? Would you feel more or less empowered to speak up at work? Would you feel more or less safe walking alone at night? How would the change affect your choices?

If society will not admit of woman's free development, then society must be remodeled.

Elizabeth Blackwell (1821–1910), first woman in the United States to earn a medical degree

Growing up, what did you learn from your family about people outside your community? What did you learn about people who were different from yourself? Describe how your feelings and beliefs have—or have not—changed over time.

You only have to look back five years to see a different world and, by extension, tangible proof that culture is ours to shape, if we try.

Lindy West (b. 1982), author and activist

THE
FUTURE
IS
FEMALE

What are the boxes that society puts you in?
Black? White? Immigrant? Woman? Write down the
preconceptions associated with each. Then make a list
of how you break or exceed those stereotypes.

Don't just talk about
it—do something.

"Women's rights are human rights."

Hillary Rodham Clinton (b. 1947),
former US senator and secretary of state

When have you been victimized in your life?
When have you victimized another?

＂

＂

Have you ever been stopped by the police?
How did you expect to be treated, and how were
you treated? If you were in the officer's shoes,
what would you have done differently?

....

....

....

....

....

....

....

....

....

....

....

....

....

....

....

....

....

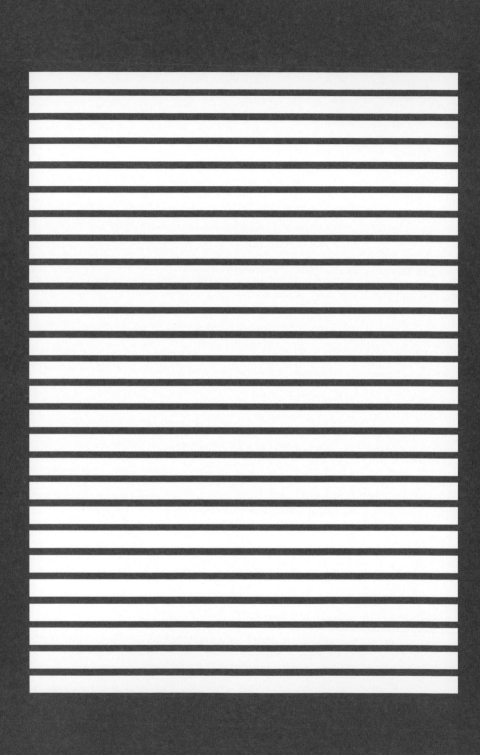

WHAT IS A CAUSE THAT YOU BELIEVE IN?

Are you interested in women's rights? Immigrant rights? LGBTQ rights? Racial equality? Climate change? Write about something that concerns you. What is the change you want to see? What are some ways that you can help? You can find a list of resources to get you started in the back of this journal.

The stars we are given.
The constellations we make.

Rebecca Solnit
(b. 1961), writer

Go to a demonstration or protest. Your voice and physical presence make a difference!

Write about a time in your life when you may have behaved in a racist way or experienced racist behavior. Describe your thoughts, feelings, and actions in detail.

"

Fight like a girl.

"

Sign at one of the women's marches, 1/21/2017

Where in society do you experience disempowerment?
What are some ways in which you might have
internalized that disempowerment?

66

Burst down those closet
doors once and for all, and
stand up and start to fight.

99

Harvey Milk (1930–1978), first
openly gay person to be elected
to public office in California

66

Now all we need is to
continue to speak the truth
fearlessly, and we shall add
to our number those who
will turn the scale to the
side of equal and full justice
in all things.

99

Lucy Stone (1818–1893),
activist and abolitionist

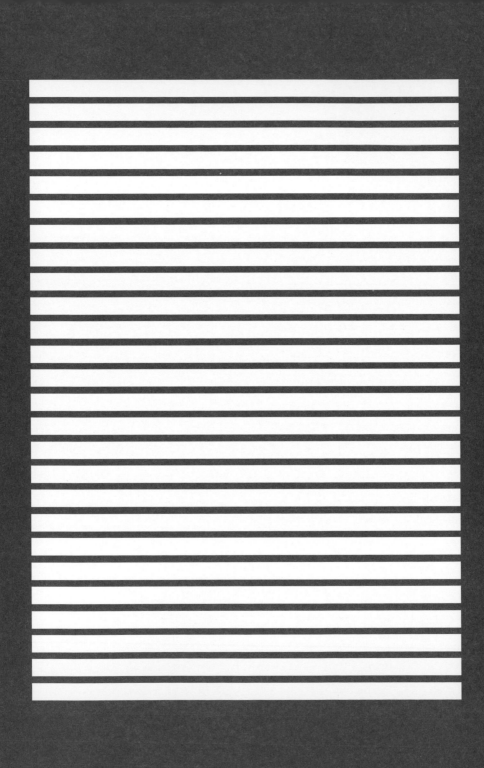

First they came for the Muslims, and we said, HELL NO!

Sign at a protest against the 1/27/17 travel ban

> **"**
> The secret of our success is that we never, never give up.
> **"**
>
> Wilma Mankiller
> (1945–2010), first female chief
> of the Cherokee Nation

"

"

SIGN OR START A PETITION.

From asking local stores to stock ethical brands to petitioning the government for clean water rights, there are many causes to get behind. What do you feel strongly about?

WHAT MAKES YOU ANGRY?

> **"**
>
> Come to me now, and loosen me from blunt agony. Labor and fill my heart with fire. Stand by me and be my ally.
>
> **"**
>
> Sappho (ca. 610–ca. 570 BCE), Greek lyric poet

There are still so many causes worth sacrificing for. There is still so much history yet to be made.

Michelle Obama (b. 1964), lawyer and activist

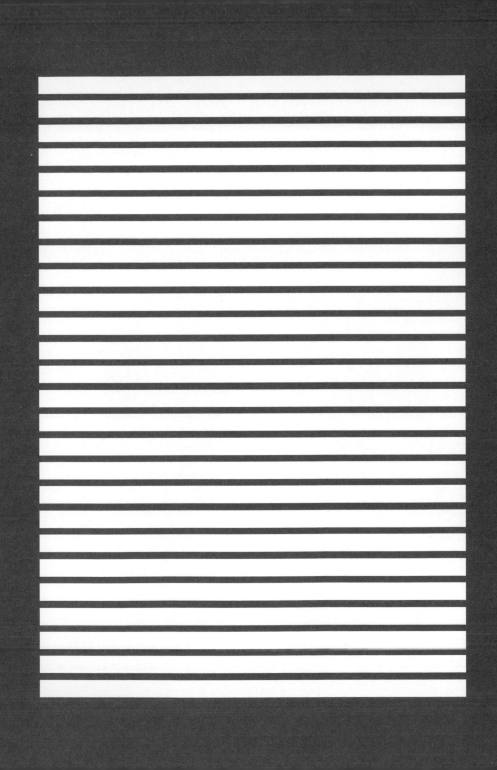

"

The truth
will set you
free, but first
it will piss
you off.

"

Gloria Steinem (b. 1934), activist and writer

Write about a time when you saw something that was wrong and said nothing. What prevented you from getting involved? Describe a time when you saw something that was wrong and did something about it.

> **"**
>
> When I get mad, you know
> that I open my big mouth.
>
> **"**
>
> Josephine Baker
> (1906–1975), entertainer

Though the sex to which I belong is considered weak, you will nevertheless find me a rock that bends to no wind.

Elizabeth I (1533–1603), former queen of England

I'm with her.

Write about a time in your life when you may
have behaved in an anti-Semitic way or experienced
anti-Semitic behavior. Describe your thoughts,
feelings, and actions in detail.

Difficult times often bring out the best in people.

Bernie Sanders (b. 1941), US senator

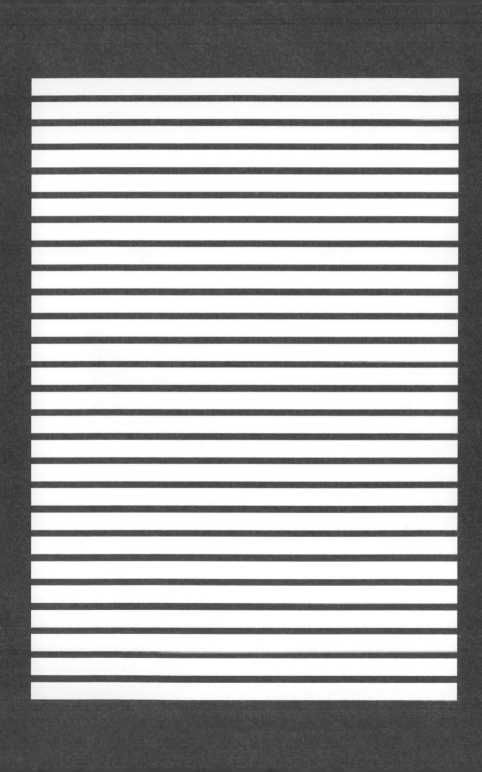

I AM NOT FREE WHILE ANY WOMAN IS UNFREE.

Audre Lorde (1934–1992), writer and activist

66

What has man ever done
that woman, under the same
advantages, could not do?

99

Ernestine Rose (1810–1892),
abolitionist and activist

Write about a time in your life when you may have behaved in an Islamophobic way or experienced Islamophobic behavior. Describe your thoughts, feelings, and actions in detail.

> **" We can do this every weekend, asshole. "**
>
> Sign at a San Francisco
> "No Ban, No Wall" rally, 2/4/17

TRUTH IS POWERFUL AND IT PREVAILS.

Sojourner Truth (ca. 1797–1883), abolitionist and activist

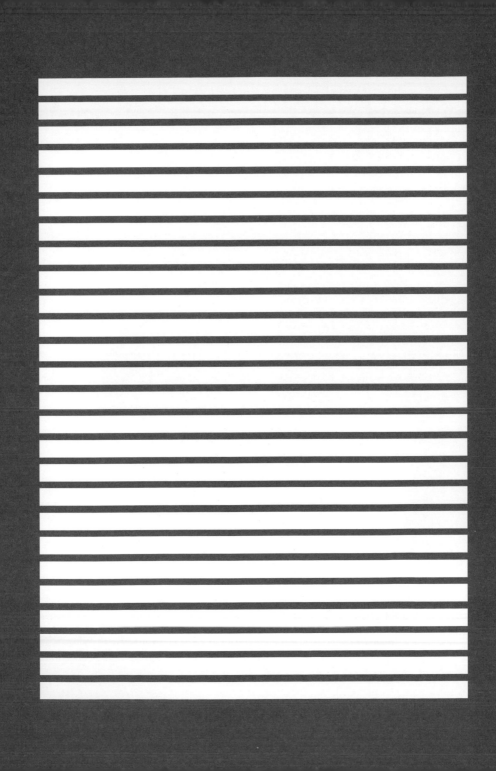

There is no freedom without a free press. Support journalism by subscribing to local and national media organizations.

> **"**
>
> ## The greatest danger to our future is apathy.
>
> **"**
>
> Jane Goodall (b. 1934),
> primatologist and
> UN Messenger of Peace

#ShePersisted

What sort of female role models did you have
when you were younger? Write about a woman
who had a positive impact on you.

> "
> *If they don't give you a seat at the table, bring a folding chair.*
> "

Shirley Chisholm (1924–2005), first African American congresswoman, and first woman and first African American to make a bid for the nomination of a major party for the US presidency

"

"

"

The American dream belongs to all of us.

"

Kamala Harris (b. 1964), US senator,
and first woman and first African American to
serve as attorney general of California

Write about an injustice that you witness on a regular basis.
What is one thing you can do to fight it?

> **"**
>
> Use your pain.
> Use your fear. Get mad.
>
> **"**
>
> Sherman Alexie
> (b. 1966), author

VOLUNTEER YOUR TIME.

By doing so, not only will you help your community, but you'll also see a different side of it and meet people you might not otherwise meet.

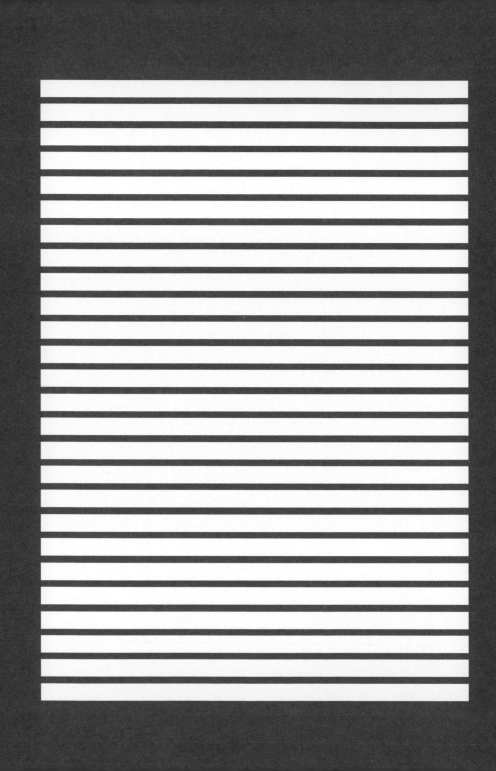

I spend all day figuring out how to beat the machine and knock the crap out of the political power structure.

Bella Abzug (1920–1998), former US congresswoman

DON'T TELL ME WHAT TO DO.

Sign at one of the women's marches, 1/21/2017

When the whole world
is silent, even one voice
becomes powerful.

Malala Yousafzai (b. 1997),
activist and youngest
Nobel Peace laureate

Equality of rights under the law shall not be denied or abridged by the United States or by any State on account of sex.

Equal Rights Amendment, introduced by suffragist Alice Paul in 1923 and passed by Congress in 1972. As of now, it still has not been ratified by fifteen states.

Power
to the

RESIST.

Sign at one of the women's marches, 1/21/17

_____

_____

_____

_____

_____

_____

_____

_____

_____

_____

_____

_____

_____

_____

_____

_____

_____

_____

_____

_____

What power and privilege might you have because of
your class, race, gender, or sexual identity? Write about a
time in your life when you benefited from that privilege.

NO, I DO NOT WEEP AT THE WORLD—I AM TOO BUSY SHARPENING MY OYSTER KNIFE.

Zora Neale Hurston (1891–1960), author and anthropologist

" I am not afraid . . . I was born to do this. "

Joan of Arc
(ca. 1412–1431), warrior and Catholic saint

Write about a time in your life when you may have behaved in a homophobic way or experienced homophobic behavior. Describe your thoughts, feelings, and actions in detail.

CONSIDER WHAT HAS KEPT YOU FROM VOLUNTEERING FOR A CAUSE YOU CARE ABOUT.

Make a list of the reasons, no matter how uncomfortable they are. Then make a list of how you can overcome these obstacles. Which one will you tackle first?

> ❝
> You must do the
> thing you think you
> cannot do.
> ❞
>
> Eleanor Roosevelt
> (1884–1962), activist

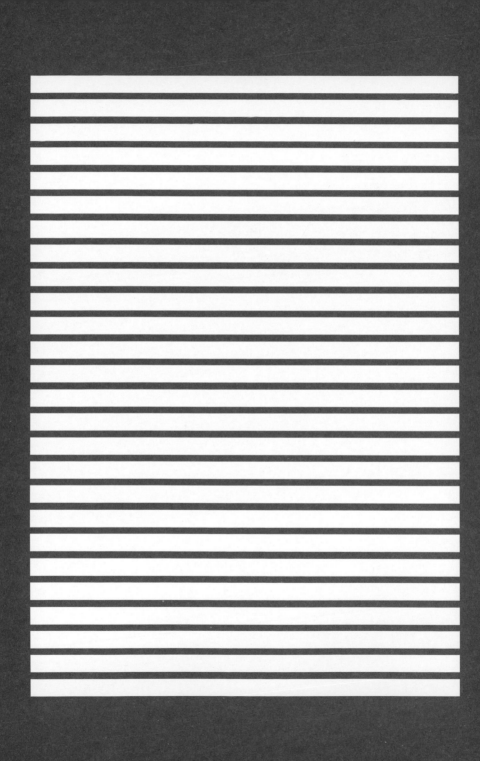

We do this because the world
we live in is a house on fire, and the
people we love are burning.

Sandra Cisneros (b. 1954), author

CALL YOUR ELECTED OFFICIALS AT THE LOCAL, STATE, OR FEDERAL LEVEL.

If they don't answer or their voice mail is full, then show up at a town-hall meeting and engage them face-to-face.

Write a letter to someone from the past whom you admire, someone who fought for a cause you believe in. What would you want them to know about the impact they made on your life?

We stand. Because we must protect
our children and our grandchildren.

LaDonna Brave Bull Allard, tribal historian, activist,
and Sacred Stone resistance camp cofounder

....
....
....
....
....
....
....
....
....
....
....
....
....
....
....
....
....

THERE WILL NEVER BE A NEW WORLD ORDER UNTIL WOMEN ARE A PART OF IT.

Alice Paul (1885–1977), women's rights activist

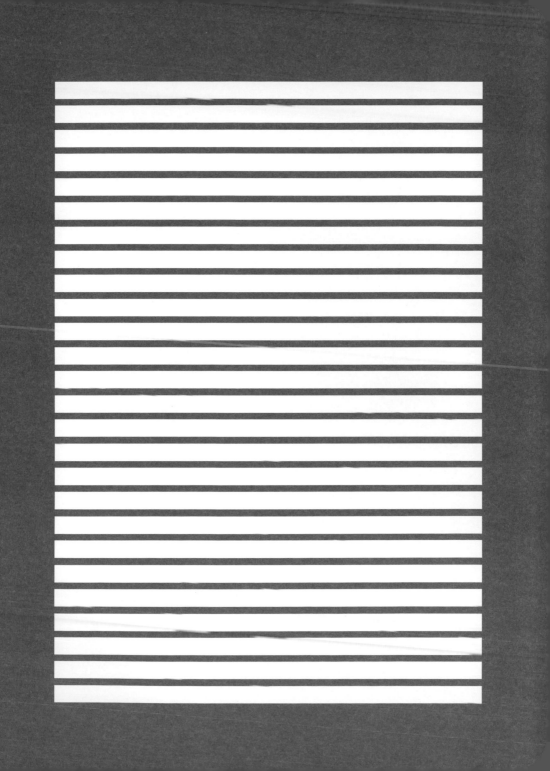

> ❝
>
> Change will not come if we
> wait for some other person
> or if we wait for some other
> time. We are the ones we've
> been waiting for. We are
> the change that we seek.
>
> ❞
>
> Barack Obama (b. 1961),
> 44th president of the United States

IMAGINE YOURSELF ON YOUR 100TH BIRTHDAY.

What advice or insight would you want to impart
to someone who is the age you are today?
What kind of role model would you like to be in the
years between now and then?

> I am not fighting for my kingdom and my wealth. I am fighting as an ordinary person for my lost freedom, my bruised body, and my outraged daughters.

Boudicca (d. 60 CE),
Celtic warrior queen

"

I can't believe we still have to protest this shit.

"

Sign at one of the women's marches, 1/21/2017

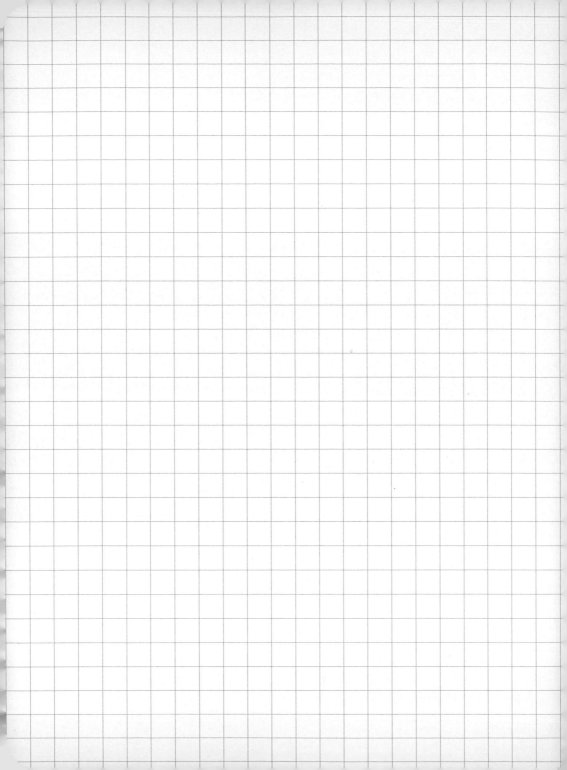

COMMIT TO A CAUSE.

A single donation can help, and consistent donations can help even more—many organizations have the option of signing up to make automatic monthly contributions.

"

"

> **"**
> The way to right
> wrongs is to turn
> the light of
> truth upon them.
> **"**
>
> Ida B. Wells-Barnett
> (1862–1931),
> journalist and activist

THERE ARE VERY FEW JOBS THAT ACTUALLY REQUIRE A PENIS OR VAGINA.

Florynce Kennedy (1916–2000), lawyer and activist

> **"**
> *There is no force equal to a woman determined to rise.*
> **"**
>
> W. E. B. Du Bois (1868–1963), author, activist, and first African American to earn a PhD from Harvard

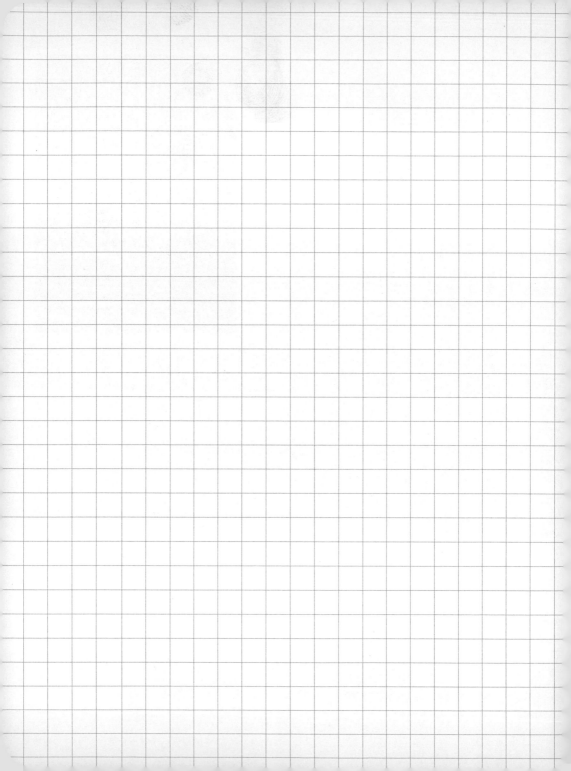

Run for office. Who knows— someday you could be POTUS.

Resources for Nasty Women

There are many resources for people ready to get their hands dirty for the sake of equality. This is by no means an exhaustive list, but I hope that it will get you started. If you find an organization in your community that sounds like something you connect to, look the group up on a charity watch website to make sure it's legit. Good luck, and keep fighting—the world needs you!

CHARITY WATCH LISTS

Charity Navigator (charitynavigator.org)
GiveWell (givewell.org)
CharityWatch (charitywatch.org)
ProPublica's Nonprofit Explorer (projects.propublica.org/nonprofits)
Women's Funding Network (womensfundingnetwork.org)

WOMEN'S HEALTH, REPRODUCTIVE RIGHTS, AND SAFETY

NARAL Pro-Choice America (naral.org)
Guttmacher Institute (guttmacher.org)
Planned Parenthood (plannedparenthood.org)

Breast Cancer Research Foundation (bcrfcure.org)

Hollaback! (ihollaback.org)

Rape, Abuse & Incest National Network (rainn.org)

National Coalition Against Domestic Violence (ncadv.org)

Coalition to Stop Gun Violence (csgv.org)

Moms Demand Action for Gun Sense in America (momsdemandaction.org)

CIVIL RIGHTS, LEGAL SERVICES, AND REFORM

Black Lives Matter (blacklivesmatter.com)

National Association for the Advancement of Colored People (naacp.org)

Her Justice (herjustice.org)

National Partnership for Women & Families (nationalpartnership.org)

National Women's Law Center (nwlc.org)

Disability Rights Education and Defense Fund (dredf.org)

Lambda Legal (lambdalegal.org)

Sylvia Rivera Law Project (srlp.org)

Human Rights Campaign (hrc.org)

GLBTQ Legal Advocates & Defenders (glad.org)

National LGBTQ Task Force (thetaskforce.org)

American Civil Liberties Union (aclu.org)

Native American Rights Fund (narf.org)

Council on American-Islamic Relations (cair.com)

Anti-Defamation League (adl.org)

Southern Poverty Law Center (splcenter.org)

National Organization for Women Foundation (now.org)

Ms. Foundation for Women (forwomen.org)

American Association of University Women (aauw.org)

YWCA (ywca.org)

IMMIGRATION

International Rescue Committee (rescue.org)

Border Angels (borderangels.org)

National Immigration Law Center (nilc.org)
National Immigration Forum (immigrationforum.org)
Young Center for Immigrant Children's Rights (theyoungcenter.org)

INTERNATIONAL ADVOCACY

Days for Girls (daysforgirls.org)
Tostan (tostan.org)
Girls Not Brides (girlsnotbrides.org)
Women on Wings (womenonwings.com)
Camfed (camfed.org)
Population Services International (psi.org)
Alliance for International Women's Rights (aiwr.org)
Women for Women International (womenforwomen.org)
Malala Fund (malala.org)
V-Day (vday.org)
Oxfam (oxfam.org)
Human Rights Watch (hrw.org)
Amnesty International (amnesty.org/en)

VOTING AND RUNNING FOR OFFICE

She Should Run (sheshouldrun.org)
League of Women Voters (lwv.org)
Emily's List (emilyslist.org)
VoteRunLead (voterunlead.org)
IGNITE (ignitenational.org)
Maggie's List (maggieslist.org)
Emerge America (emergeamerica.org)
Run for Something (runforsomething.net)
Wellstone (wellstone.org)
Gay & Lesbian Victory Institute (victoryinstitute.org)
Higher Heights for America (higherheightsforamerica.org)
New American Leaders Project (newamericanleaders.org)

EDUCATION

National Center for Science Education (ncse.com)
500 Women Scientists (500womenscientists.org)
Girls on the Run (girlsontherun.org)
Girls Who Code (girlswhocode.com)
Boys & Girls Clubs of America (bgca.org)

CLIMATE CHANGE

350.org (350.org)
Earthjustice (earthjustice.org)
NextGen Climate (nextgenclimate.org)
Sierra Club (sierraclub.org)
Union of Concerned Scientists (ucsusa.org)
Greenpeace (greenpeace.org)

THE MEDIA

Women, Action & the Media (womenactionmedia.org)
Women in Media & News (wimnonline.org)
Committee to Protect Journalists (cpj.org)
PEN America (pen.org)
Reporters Committee for Freedom of the Press (rcfp.org)

CURRENT EVENTS

New York Times (nytimes.com)
Wall Street Journal (wsj.com)
New Yorker (newyorker.com)
Economist (economist.com)
Atlantic (theatlantic.com)
Bloomberg (bloomberg.com)
National Public Radio (npr.org)
British Broadcasting Corporation (bbc.com)

About the Author

Before committing to the world of books, Anna Katz had a career in mental health and social services. As an editor and writer at Girl Friday Productions, she has worked with National Geographic Kids, Deloitte, and Pokémon, among others. Her newest book, *Swimming Holes of Washington*, will be published by Mountaineers Books in 2018.

DEFY

PERSIST

RESOLVE